Contents

KU-639-804

British and Jewish

Around 276,000 Jewish men, women and children live in Britain today. They form one of Britain's smallest communities – making up less than one per cent of the total population. There are in Britain now about 150,000 fewer people identifying themselves as Jews than there were around 1950.

Being 'Jewish' does not mean the same thing for all people. Some Jews use the name to describe only their ethnic origins, some use it to describe their religious faith and some to describe a combination of their faith and their ancestry.

Different backgrounds

Jewish people in Britain are descended from families who lived in the Middle East thousands of years ago. But their customs and traditions are not all the same. In the 1st century CE, Jewish families were expelled from their Middle Eastern homeland. They settled in many parts of Europe and North Africa, where they developed different lifestyles and spoke different languages. When they arrived to settle in Britain, they brought these local differences with them.

Jewish boys cross a busy road in London on their way to school. Most British Jews live in London, or nearby.

JEWS
IN BRITAIN

Fiona Macdonald

Consultant: Ephraim Borowski

Photography by Chris Fairclough

FRANKLIN WATTS

LONDON • SYDNEY

First published in 2005 by
Franklin Watts
96 Leonard Street
London
EC2A 4XD

Franklin Watts Australia
45-51 Huntley Street
Alexandria
NSW 2015

A CIP catalogue record for this book
is available from the British Library
Dewey Classification: 305.6'96'041

Planning and production by Discovery Books Limited
Editor: Kate Taylor
Designer: Rob Norridge

Photographic acknowledgements: P4, David Kampfner/Life File Photos/
Photographers Direct; P6, Hulton Archive/Getty Images; P7 (t), W. and
D. Downey/Mansell/ Time Life Pictures/Getty Images; P7 (b), Corbis;
P9, Corbis; P10, David Kampfner/Life File Photos/Photographers Direct;
P16, Corbis; P18, Des Gershon/CIPL/ Photographers Direct; P19, World
Religions Photo Library/Photographers Direct; P20, University of
Glasgow; P22, Topham Picture Point; P23, Frank Trapper/Corbis; P26,
David Savill/Getty Images; P27, David Hoffman Photo Library/Alamy/
Photographers Direct. All others supplied by Chris Fairclough

ISBN: 0 7496 5888 6

Printed in Dubai

Life in Britain

Today, Jewish people play a very important part in British life. They hold top positions in business, finance and science. They have careers as scholars, or in entertainment and the arts. In towns and cities, many Jewish men and women serve as local councillors, welfare workers and community volunteers.

Inside one of Britain's 365 synagogues. Local Jews come here to attend services or to pray alone.

"We may not be the majority in Britain but if you try, you will be able to carry on a Jewish way of life and pass on your knowledge to other people...

Jewish school student.

Charity work

Jewish people have also worked hard to improve life in Britain by campaigning to change laws, and fundraising for good causes. Three of Britain's leading charitable organisations – Amnesty International, the RSPCA and Childline – were founded or led by Jews.

British Jews celebrate all of the same festivals as Jews in other parts of the world. These children are dressed up for Purim, a happy festival celebrated with music, dancing, parties and funny costumes.

Arriving and settling

Jews may have come to Britain almost 2000 years ago, with occupying Roman armies. William the Conqueror brought Jewish men to Britain from France, soon after 1066.

For the next 200 years, small communities of Jewish people lived in British towns, as traders and moneylenders. But Christian religious ideas, and jealousy of Jewish wealth, led to attacks on Jewish families. In 1290, all Jewish people were ordered out of England by King Edward I.

Sephardic Jews

In 1656 Jews were officially allowed to live in England again. They opened a new synagogue (place of worship) in London the same year. Most of these Jewish settlers came from southern Europe and North Africa. Known as 'Sephardic' Jews, they spoke Spanish or Italian. They settled in London or along the south coast.

Jews were often moneylenders or bankers in Medieval Europe as Christians were not meant to profit from lending money to others.

Ashkenazi Jews

From around 1750, they were followed by German-speaking 'Ashkenazi' Jews, from Central Europe. These families settled further north, in Birmingham, Manchester and Liverpool. More Jews from Central Europe arrived in the early 19th century, to escape political unrest in their home countries.

Immigrants

The largest number of Jewish immigrants – over 120,000 – arrived from Russia and Eastern Europe between 1881 and 1914. Most spoke Yiddish and were fleeing government persecution. In the 1930s, Jews from Germany and nearby lands came to Britain to escape Hitler's brutal Nazi regime. The Nazis' extreme anti-Semitic policies led to the systematic murder of 6,000,000 European Jews.

Benjamin Disraeli, later Lord Beaconsfield, became Britain's first prime minister of Jewish ancestry in 1868. He was re-elected in 1874.

Sick, shivering and starving, these Jewish men were some of the few to survive the terrible Nazi concentration camp, at Ebensee, Austria, during World War II (1939–1945).

The Jewish faith

Judaism is an ancient faith. It was first taught by Abraham, the founder of the Hebrew people who lived in the Middle East over 4000 years ago. Abraham believed that there was one God, who created the world. God had chosen the Hebrews, and made a promise to them. If they worshipped Him, He would look after them, and give them a homeland. Later, God would send a Messiah (an annointed king), to set up His kingdom on earth.

Moses

The Hebrews were originally a small family group living in Canaan (later to become Israel). Due to famine they were forced to move to Egypt, where they lived for 210 years, becoming the Egyptians' slaves. Moses led them out of Egypt. On their journey, he received the Torah (teachings) from God. Included in it were the Ten Commandments and 613 Mitzvot (laws). After Moses' death, Joshua became leader and led the Jews back to Israel.

Learning to read the Torah. Jewish people use a pointer, called a yad ('hand'), to avoid touching the parchment.

The Torah

The Torah is still the basis of Jewish life and worship today. A sidrah (a passage from it) is read out in synagogues every week, throughout the year. Most Jewish homes have a mezuzah (a small parchment scroll usually contained in a decorative box affixed to a doorpost) as a reminder to obey God's laws. It contains the first lines of the Shema, a passage from the Torah.

THE TEN COMMANDMENTS

1. **Do not worship any god except God.**
2. **Do not make any idols (images) of God.**
3. **Do not misuse God's name.**
4. **Keep the Shabbat (day of rest) holy.**
5. **Honour your father and mother.**
6. **Do not murder.**
7. **Do not commit adultery.**
8. **Do not steal.**
9. **Do not tell lies.**
10. **Do not covet (envy and long for) other people's possessions.**

The Talmud

The Torah was taught in two ways – the written Torah (the Bible) and the oral Torah, which was written down later and formed the basis of the Talmud. This contains laws and guidance on: how to say prayers, meet for worship, celebrate festivals, live in communities and punish criminals; as well as laws of marriage and Jewish family and daily life.

The Western Wall, in Jerusalem, Israel, is the only surviving part of the ancient Jewish Temple. Jewish people from all over the world visit it to pray. Some write their prayers on paper and put them into cracks in the Wall.

Living as a Jew

Over the centuries, different groups within the Jewish community have come to follow their faith in different ways. Orthodox Jews obey Torah and Talmud laws precisely. But Progressive Jews (also known as Reform and Liberal Jews) believe that these laws can be adapted to suit changing conditions.

Orthodox tradition

Most British Jews belong to Orthodox synagogues. But there are also ultra-Orthodox and very Liberal communities. A survey taken in Britain in 1999 found that both these groups were growing, but that numbers were falling among the moderate majority.

Orthodox Jews do not travel in motor vehicles during Shabbat, they choose to walk instead.

Shabbat

For most Jews, the two most important observances are Shabbat (day of rest) and Kashrut (food laws). Shabbat is a holy day celebrated on Friday evenings and Saturday. Most Jewish people like to share it with their families and friends. They try not to work, but spend the time restfully. Progressive Jews may visit friends or family who live nearby, or watch or take part in sport. Strict Orthodox families may refuse to cook, travel or even switch on electric lights, because that would break God's commandment.

A challah loaf of sweet bread, eaten at Shabbat. Traditionally, the dough for challah loaves is plaited, or arranged in another decorative shape, to show that it is special.

Shabbat begins on Friday evening, at sunset. Women light two candles, and say a prayer over them. Challah (sweet bread) and wine, which form part of a family meal, are blessed. Men may go to prayers at the synagogue before or after this meal; there are also Saturday services for the whole family to attend.

Prayer clothes

Orthodox men wear a yarmulka (skull-cap) and tallit (white wool prayer shawl, with black or purple stripes), to show obedience to and respect for God. They may also wear tefillin (small leather boxes, containing Torah texts). Orthodox women cover their hair with a hat, a scarf or a wig.

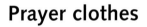

Many Jewish men and boys choose to wear a kippah or yarmulka (skull-cap). They believe that covering the head shows respect for God.

Women in synagogues

In Orthodox synagogues, women cannot lead prayers or be rabbis (leaders), although there are many female teachers, and men and women worshippers usually sit apart. However, Progressive synagogues in Britain have appointed women to lead prayers and guide worshippers since 1977, when Julia Neuberger became Britain's first female rabbi.

Food, festivals and fasting

For many Jews, obeying food laws (Kashrut) is an essential part of Jewish lifestyle. Serving Kosher (permitted) food is a way of drawing closer to God.

Kosher food

Jewish food laws are strict. Pork and shellfish are banned, and only certain birds may be eaten. Animals must be killed in accordance with strict Kashrut procedures, so that as much blood as possible is removed from the body. Animals that have died from old age or disease are never eaten. Meat and milk cannot be cooked or eaten together, or served on the same dishes. Orthodox Jewish homes have two sets of kitchenware – and even two dishwashers – to avoid contamination.

Kosher food stores can be found in most large towns in Britain, and some areas, like Golders Green in London, have kosher bakeries, supermarkets, cafés, delicatessens and restaurants offering kosher food.

Shopping for a kosher meal. In London and other major British cities, there are supermarkets specialising in kosher food and traditional Jewish ingredients.

Keep fit
According to Jewish ethics, the human being is a custodian, not an owner, of the body. As such, one is obliged to keep it in good condition.

Rabbi Rapoport, spokesman for the Chief Rabbi of the UK.

Apples dipped in honey are eaten at Rosh Hashanah. Their sweetness represents wishes for a happy and pleasant New Year.

Bagels and borsht

Kosher food in Britain has a rich heritage. Settlers from many parts of Europe, North Africa and the Middle East have all contributed to a fine multicultural tradition. Any style of food can be kosher if it complies with the rules. Favourites include bagels, cheesecake, blintzes (little pancakes), gefilte fish (minced fish patties), latkes (potato cakes), borsht (beetroot soup) and falafel (spiced, fried chickpea nuggets). Bagels have become a popular food among people from all backgrounds and can now be found in supermarkets, food stores and bakeries throughout Britain.

Special foods

During the festival of Pesach (Passover), which remembers Moses' journey out of Egypt, special foods are eaten. They include bitter herbs, eggs, matzot (unleavened bread) and charoset (chopped apples and nuts mixed with wine and spices). Many Jews fast all day on Yom Kippur, when Jewish people remember their sins and ask for God's forgiveness.

Pesach is celebrated with a special meal, called 'seder', and by telling stories and singing songs about Moses.

A Jewish home

Most British Jews, like people throughout the world, believe that family life is important. They say that a loving, caring family can help members live good lives, and benefit their communities. Families can work together, building up businesses, or supporting each other in times of crisis.

Local community

In the past, many Jewish families in Britain lived close together in the same inner-city districts. They wanted to be near other people who followed the same faith and shared similar traditions. They set up shops that sold kosher foods, and Hebrew books and newspapers.

Today, many Jewish families have moved out of big cities to the suburbs but almost one in five Jews in Britain live in the borough of Barnet in London. Fifteen per cent of Barnet's population are Jewish, which is reflected in the synagogues, religious schools, social clubs, community centres, shops, restaurants and Jewish charities found there.

Jewish women are honoured because they create homes where families can live according to Jewish traditions. They also pass on Jewish prayers, songs, games, customs – and recipes – to the next generation.

Jewish newspapers, written in English and published in the UK, keep British Jews in touch with each other, and with other Jewish communities around the world.

Changing times

Jewish family life is changing. Increasingly, young Jewish people in Britain are 'marrying out' of the community. Jewish men and women are choosing partners from other faiths, or none. Unless their partner converts to Judaism, it is very difficult for them to create a thoroughly Jewish home.

Orthodox Jewish leaders feel that this is damaging. They offer counselling and marriage guidance, for support. Orthodox women often have large numbers of children, which helps keep Britain's Jewish community alive.

GOLDERS GREEN

There are Jewish communities throughout Britain. The largest and most well known is found in Golders Green, in Barnet in North London. The High Road there is packed with kosher restaurants, bakeries, butchers, supermarkets, Jewish bookstores and gift shops. There are also dozens of synagogues in the area. Nearby Hendon, also in Barnet, is home to the Hasmonean and Independent schools, as well as the Yakar, a synagogue known for its lecture series.

Children and growing up

Traditionally, Jewish identity is passed from a mother to her children. But some Progressive rabbis (leaders) in Britain accept children with non-Jewish mothers into the faith community, so long as their Jewish fathers promise to bring them up as Jews.

Birth

The birth of a Jewish baby is greeted with congratulations. A boy is circumcised at around 8 days old, and given a Hebrew religious name. The birth of a girl is announced in the synagogue, and the community says prayers for her. Some Progressive synagogues hold a modern ceremony, Brit Rechitza, when they wash a baby girl's feet as a sign of welcome.

> **Life is split into two as the majority of my friends aren't Jewish, and so don't understand why I miss school sometimes for festivals, or have to miss going out shopping to go to a service....Hopefully, being an 'active' Jew will still be a large part of my life when I'm older.**
>
> *Jewish schoolchild.*

Bar Mitzvahs and Bat Mitzvahs

When a boy is 13 years old, he becomes an adult in a ceremony known as 'Bar Mitzvah'. On the first Shabbat after his birthday, he goes to the synagogue, puts on a tallit, reads or chants a passage from the Torah and is blessed. He is then a full member of the Jewish community. A similar 'Bat Mitzvah' ceremony is held when a girl reaches 12. Both are celebrated with large family parties.

Reading the Torah at a Bar Mitzvah ceremony. The Torah is written in Hebrew, the language of the ancient Hebrew people, and of the modern state of Israel today.

Education

Many Jewish families value education highly. They live close to top state schools, with good teachers and facilities, or pay school fees to educate their children privately. As a result, Jewish people are the most highly-educated in Britain. Over 37 per cent have a university degree.

Religious schools

From around 3 to 15 years old, many Jewish children in Britain also attend religious schools, linked to synagogues. These schools teach Jewish history, the Hebrew language and the Jewish faith. They arrange educational trips and parties at Jewish festivals. Other Jewish youth organisations arrange summer camps, workshops, sports events and discos. They teach young people about Israel (the modern Jewish state, and ancient Jewish homeland), and encourage exchange visits with Israeli teenagers. There are Jewish Brownie groups and a Jewish Lads and Girls Brigade.

These children go to a Jewish school. As well as typical subjects, they take extra classes that teach them about Judaism and how to be a good Jew.

Weddings and funerals

Most Jewish men and women hope to get married and have children. They believe this is God's law. The Torah and the Talmud teach that married people should be faithful and understanding to each other.

Arranged marriages

In the past, marriages were arranged by parents, sometimes helped by a match-maker. But today, most Jewish people in Britain choose their own partners. They may meet at Jewish social gatherings or community activities, or be introduced by friends and relatives. There are also Jewish websites offering to help find partners. Many Jewish men and women wait to finish their education or establish their careers before deciding to marry.

Weddings

At a Jewish wedding, the bride and groom dress traditionally, in a long white frock with a veil and a smart black suit. They stand under a chuppah (canopy), which represents heaven, and is a sign of God's presence. The rabbi, using a cup of wine, says prayers and the marriage contract is read out. After further prayers, the bride and groom share the cup of wine that has been blessed, and then the groom crushes a wineglass under his foot. Ceremonies are usually held in one of Britain's synagogues. However, as long as a rabbi is present, and there is a chuppah, they can be held anywhere.

At a Jewish wedding, the bride and groom stand under a chuppah (canopy). It is a symbol of the sky, and of heaven, and a sign that God is all around.

Funerals

Jewish burials are traditionally held within 24 hours of death. Each Jewish community in Britain has its own burial society, called a Chavra Kadisha, which helps the family make the funeral arrangements and prepare the body for burial. Jews are buried in a Jewish cemetery, where the family and friends congregate for the service.

A small tear (keriah) is often made in the mourners' clothes, representing a broken heart, and a eulogy is given by a rabbi. A year of official mourning follows the death.

Graves at a Jewish cemetery. Some are decorated with traditional Jewish symbols, such as a six-pointed star. The names of the dead are carved in Hebrew letters on some headstones, too.

Focus on Glasgow

Glasgow, in west-central Scotland, is the largest Scottish city. About 630,000 people live there. Once world famous for industry and ship-building, it is now a regional capital, with universities, museums, art galleries and busy shopping areas and offices. Its magnificent old buildings and vibrant cultural life make it a popular tourist destination. It is also home to Britain's fourth-largest Jewish community.

Jews in Scotland

There are about 6,400 Jewish people in Scotland – 0.13 per cent of the Scottish population. Most live in Glasgow. Jews have settled there since around 1740, when they helped develop international trade. The first Jewish scholar graduated from Glasgow University in 1787, and the first synagogue was built (at Garnethill) in 1823.

Glasgow University – one of the oldest and most famous in Britain. Jewish students have studied there for over 200 years.

> "Glasgow New Synagogue ... offers a vision of Judaism which is fresh and relevant and a friendly environment for its members to share in religious, social and educational activities. If you're looking for a Judaism which finds a balance between tradition and modernity – this is it!

Glasgow New Synagogue (Newton Mearns) spokesman.

Synagogues, charities and clubs

Today, there are six synagogues in and around Glasgow. Five are Orthodox. There is also a Mikveh – ritual bath – used by some Orthodox women, and a large number of Jewish charities, cultural and artistic clubs, adult education classes, welfare services, children's groups, Israeli support organisations and other community activities. The last specialist kosher butcher closed in 2001, but several shops stock kosher food.

The Orthodox synagogue at Giffnock & Newlands welcomes worshippers from all over the Glasgow area. Some people travel long distances to pray there, because there are no Jewish places of worship in their own small villages and towns.

The sign of a Jewish youth club set up in Glasgow and run by local Jewish volunteers.

Newton Mearns

Newton Mearns is a wealthy commuter village, about 10km from Glasgow centre. It has two of Glasgow's synagogues, one of which is the home of Scotland's Reform Jewish community. In the late 20th century, many of Glasgow's Jewish families moved out of the city to quieter, cleaner, less crowded environments. Newton Mearns is typical of these.

Jewish people at work

Jewish people have achieved success in all areas of British life, but especially in business, science, fashion, entertainment and the media. Many of Britain's largest and best-known retail companies have been founded and run by Jewish entrepreneurs. They include Marks and Spencer and Tesco.

Small businesses

Jews also own and manage many smaller companies. Around 30 per cent of Jewish people in Britain run their own businesses, compared with a national average of around 10 per cent. Jewish men and women have some of the lowest unemployment rates in Britain – less than 5 per cent of those seeking employment are unable to find a job. Among employees, Jewish men are more likely than people of any other faith to work in banking, finance or insurance.

This shop in London sells fresh fruit and vegetables. It is typical of many small, family-run Jewish businesses.

Scientists

Jewish scientists from Britain have won 13 Nobel Prizes – one of the world's top honours for science – in the last 60 years. Other Jewish experts include Lord Winston, who has pioneered new fertility treatments, Oliver Sacks, who has explored the brain, and Susan Greenfield, who has investigated its chemistry. They have all won praise for their ability to explain scientific ideas to the public.

WOMEN AND WORK

Around one third of all Jewish women of working age have no job outside the home. This is mostly because they are fully occupied caring for children or elderly relatives, like many other women in Britain. However, a large number of Jewish women have achieved success in Britain in careers ranging from secretaries to movie stars!

British actress Rachel Weisz, who is Jewish, arrives at a glittering awards ceremony in London.

Celebrating
and entertaining

Like other Britons, Jewish people enjoy entertaining their friends, neighbours and colleagues, or going out to theatres, cinemas and sporting events. Jewish families and friends celebrate many occasions, such as getting a new job, or passing exams, that have no direct link with religion. But many other celebrations are rooted in the Jewish faith.

Happy New Year

Rosh Hashanah and Yom Kippur

Two very important festivals in the Jewish calendar are Rosh Hashanah (New Year) and Yom Kippur (Day of Atonement). At Rosh Hashanah, a shofar (ram's horn) is blown loudly in the synagogue, asking God to grant us all a good year. Yom Kippur, ten days later, is the day Jews ask for forgiveness.

Cards for Rosh Hashanah (Jewish New Year) are decorated with pictures of fruit – especially pomegranates – and flowers. Both are symbols of new life and hope.

Festivals

Other Jewish festivals are celebrated in more lively ways, although they still have a deep spiritual meaning. They all remind Jews of God's goodness to Jewish people in the past.

At Sukkot, families shelter in huts made of branches and decorated with fruit and flowers. Purim is celebrated with noisy, cheerful fancy-dress parties.

Making a shelter of branches for the festival of Sukkot.

Hanukkah

At Hanukkah special candles or oil lamps are burned in Jewish homes for eight days, and children often receive presents. During Hanukkah, huge menorahs (a nine-branched candle holder) are also erected throughout Britain, in places such as Golders Green and Wimbledon in London, Cannon Hill Park in Birmingham and Albert Square in Manchester. Special services are held outside.

A children's Hanukkah candle holder. Hanukkah is sometimes spelt with a single k.

JEWISH ENTERTAINERS

Talented Jewish people have made great contributions to British films, music, theatre and TV. Famous Jewish entertainers include actress Maureen Lipman, comedy writer Ben Elton, impressionist Ali G, comedian Ruby Wax and TV cook Nigella Lawson.

Threats and problems

The vast majority (over 80 per cent) of Jewish people living in Britain were born here, and have British nationality. Many belong to families who have lived in Britain for over 100 years. Even so, some Jewish people report that they do not feel fully accepted by all other Britons as equal members of the community.

Some may remember violent anti-Semitism (prejudice against Jewish people) that broke out in Britain between 1900 and 1939. Some Jews fear that it might return, more forcefully.

Fascists (right-wing supporters of Nazi Germany) attack Jewish people in London, 1938. At that time, Jews protested against Britain's friendly contacts with Hitler, the Nazi leader.

Gravestones at Hollybrook cemetery, Southampton, daubed with Nazi slogans and swastikas.

Attacks on synagogues

There are still groups in Britain who hold strong anti-Semitic views and more than 100 British synagogues have been attacked since 2000. Historic and holy Torah scrolls have been burnt, fires have been started and Nazi signs have been daubed all over graves. On police advice, some British synagogue leaders now ask visitors to provide proof of identity, before letting them into the building.

Assumptions

Some Jews in Britain get upset or angry when other Britons automatically assume that they support the actions of the state of Israel simply because Israel is a Jewish state. Many also feel threatened by some Muslim political activists in Britain who hold extreme anti-Israeli views.

> It annoys me that some people look at me and think they know everything about me – what I like and what I think – without even bothering to ask me.
>
> *Gemma Harris, Golders Green, London.*

Future hopes and fears

More than any other ethnic or religious minority in Britain, Jewish men and women have assimilated (adapted or absorbed) themselves into the local culture. From mostly poor beginnings, they have been successful and used their wealth and skills to benefit British society.

Observing your faith

Many Jewish leaders are worried that successful Jewish families will fail to observe Shabbat or holy festivals, and eventually drift away from their faith. Some younger Jewish people look for new ways of worship, or express their faith through community action – like Jewish peace campaigner Tom Handel who was tragically shot by Israeli troops while trying to help Palestinians. In 2003, a survey reported that over half of all Jewish people in Britain still felt that their faith was an important part of their identity

Lighting candles at Hanukkah. Jewish children in Britain today learn traditional customs from older family members.

A rabbi shows a young boy the scrolls of the Torah. The scrolls are protected by a richly-decorated cover.

Generations

The Jewish community in Britain is also getting older. Today, one in five of all Jewish men and women is aged 65 years or more. As a group, Jews are the oldest among all the communities in Britain.

Although younger Jewish adults are very healthy, with the lowest rate of disability (just 13 per cent) among Britons, older Jewish people naturally suffer from some of the common conditions of old age. They are more likely than all other minority groups to live alone, or with just one other pensioner. But many of these Jewish senior citizens have greatly-loved, young grandchildren. They rely on them, with hope and faith, to keep Britain's Jewish community alive.

" We may not make up a huge percentage of the population of Britain but we have great community spirit and help each other and support each other in every way we can. And we will no doubt continue to do so.

Mrs Webb, Glasgow.

Glossary

Abraham a leader of the Hebrew people who lived in the Middle East over 4000 years ago

anti-Semitic discriminating against Jewish people

challah a loaf of sweet bread eaten at Shabbat

circumcise to remove part or all of the foreskin from the penis

concentration camp a prison camp used under the rule of Hitler in Nazi Germany

custodian somebody responsible for looking after valuable property

entrepreneur someone who sets up new businesses to make a profit

ethnic belonging to a group through descent or culture

eulogy a speech praising someone

Hanukkah a Jewish festival that lasts eight days

Hebrew an official language of Israel

immigrant somebody who has moved to a country to live permanently

Israel the modern Jewish state

kosher permitted

match-maker someone who arranges marriages

Middle East the region stretching from the eastern Mediterranean to the western side of the Indian subcontinent

Moses a Hebrew prophet who is believed to have written down the Ten Commandments

Nazi a member of the German National Socialist Party, the extreme right-wing party led by Adolf Hitler that ruled Germany from 1933 to 1945

Orthodox Judaism a branch of Judaism that believes the Torah was directly handed down from God to Moses

persecution cruel or unfair treatment of people because of their ethnic origin or religious beliefs

Pesach the Jewish festival of Passover

Purim a Jewish festival which remembers part of the biblical story of Esther

rabbi a Jewish leader or teacher

Rosh Hashanah a Jewish festival celebrating the Jewish New Year

scrolls rolls of paper that have been written on

Shabbat the Jewish Sabbath, celebrated on Saturday

swastika a Nazi symbol

synagogue a Jewish place of worship

tallit a white wool prayer shawl with black or purple stripes

Talmud a collection of ancient Jewish writings

tefillin small leather boxes containing Torah texts

Ten Commandments the ten laws given to Moses by God, according to the Torah

Torah the Jewish scroll on which the first five books of the Bible are written

World War II a war fought in Europe, Africa and Asia between 1939 and 1945

yarmulka skull-cap

Yom Kippur a Jewish festival celebrating the day of Atonement

Further information

This is a selection of websites that may be useful for finding out further information on Judaism and Jews in Britain.

http://atschool.eduweb.co.uk/carolrb/judaism/judai1.html
a simple introduction to Judiasm with contributions from children

www.akhlah.com
a Jewish children's learning network

www.hitchams.suffolk.sch.uk/synagogue/index.htm
a virtual visit to a synagogue

www.geocities.com/atid10
a Jewish illustrated encyclopaedia

www.bbc.co.uk/religion/religions/judaism
a BBC site with useful links

www.jewishvirtuallibrary.org/jsource/vjw/England.html
a history of Jewish people in Britain

www.somethingjewish.co.uk
a website by Jewish people, for Jewish people, that contains everything from Jewish jokes and recipes to serious political discussions

www.jewfaq.org
a Jewish online encyclopaedia

www.jewishmuseum.org.uk
London's museum of Jewish life

Note to parents and teachers

Every effort has been made by the Publishers to ensure that these websites are suitable for children; that they are of the highest educational value, and that they contain no inappropriate or offensive material. However, because of the nature of the Internet, it is impossible to guarantee that the contents of these sites will not be altered. We strongly advise that Internet access is supervised by a responsible adult.

Index